Pegan Diet Cookbook

**Quick and Easy Pegan Recipes
Bringing the Best of
the Paleo and Vegan
Diets Together
for Healthy Eating**

Madison Miller

DISCLAIMER

Contents

INTRODUCTION

If you're thinking about going Pegan, you're thinking smart my friend because going Pegan means going clean, going fresh, and going oh so deliciously good. Peganism is the happy marriage of the Paleo and Vegan lifestyles.

The Paleo lifestyle is a throwback to eating the way our ancestors did thousands of years ago. Clearly, our Paleolithic ancestors were not noshing on Twinkies and microwave pizzas since processed foods are a relatively new invention, thanks to modern-day machinery.

Prior to processed pseudo-food, meals required foraging the land and foods were eaten fire-cooked or raw. The typical diet would have been composed of fruits, vegetables, nuts, and animal protein.

The other half of the Pegan lifestyle is composed of elements of the Vegan diet. Vegans do not consume animal proteins, nor do they consume animal products like yogurt and eggs. Instead, their diet relies heavily on clean whole foods like veggies, fruits, nuts, and grains.

In this book we have brought together the best of both worlds to introduce you to the Pegan lifestyle. The Pegan cookbook is filled with delicious recipes for breakfast, lunch, dinner, appetizers, and snacks that take into consideration all of the elements of the Pegan diet.

These dishes will keep you healthy, satiated, and glowing. Have pink grapefruit with Coconut Lime Dressing for a delicious antioxidant boost in the morning, or perhaps some Coconut Pancakes with Peaches and Walnuts for a decadent brunch on Sunday.

The lunch offerings are divine, if I do say so myself. Enjoy Pistachio Jewel Salad for a taste of the unbeknownst kind, or some Hearty Cabbage and Fennel Soup.

When the dinner bell gongs, whip out the grill and enjoy a Portabella Mushroom Salad with an appetizer of Almond Honey Cauli-Skewers.

And you won't have to skip dessert, since the offerings are healthy but also mucho delicious—like our designer Strawberry Cashew Cake.

Differences between Paleo, Pegan, Vegan

The key to the Pegan diet is the manner in which the Paleo and Vegan values are combined. The Paleo principles require followers to stick to a diet of organic meats, poultry, seafood, fruits, vegetables, nuts, and seeds. Dairy products, as well as grain products, legumes, and processed foods are not allowed on the Paleo Diet

For the vegan diet, followers can eat organic fruits, vegetables, nuts, and seeds, while eliminating all animal proteins as well as animal protein products like milk and cheese.

When combining the worlds of Paleo and Vegan, you end up with a supremely healthy table of foods to choose from. On the Pegan diet you can eat all sorts of organic fruits, vegetables, nuts, and seeds, (just like the Vegan diet), but in addition you can enjoy a limited amount of animal protein. Whereas the Paleo diet eliminates all grain products and legumes, the Pegan diet allows for limited amounts on a daily basis.

Pegan Guidelines

Fruits, Veggies

Fresh veggies and fruits are in style all the time when you're on the Pegan diet. You can enjoy tons of raw or cooked veggies—and fruits are great too—but make sure you limit fruits with high sugar like pineapple since too much sugar on any diet is not good.

Nuts and Seeds

Nuts and seeds are full of heart-healthy fats and would have been a very important part of the Paleolithic diet. Eating a small portion of nuts and seeds daily will keep you full and give you the fats you need for healthy-looking skin, hair, and nails. However, remember that it's easy to go through a large amount of nuts and seeds, and although it may seem you've only eaten a little bit, nuts have a high amount of fat packed into just one little nut. When eating nuts limit your portions.

Animal Products

Now, animal proteins are allowed on the Pegan diet, think of them the same way you would think of throwing parsley on top of a dish, essentially the animal protein is not the star player on your plate but rather it is a somewhere between a garnish and a condiment. Also remember that when you are choosing your poultry, meats, and seafood, make sure they are grain-fed or wild, respectively.

Eggs

The Pegan diet recommends that you consume 2 eggs per day in order to get essential proteins, and also to ensure you get that satiation you need so you won't feel compelled to consume unhealthy foods.

Grains and Legumes

The Paleo diet eliminates all grains and legumes, however the good thing about the Pegan diet is that you can include small portions of both in your daily diet. It is recommended that you consume ½ cup of low-glycemic grains like quinoa on a daily basis to keep you satiated. Additionally, you can enjoy up to ½ a cup of legumes on a daily basis for a protein punch.

The Pegan Difference

Eating the Pegan way means eating healthy, clean, delicious food that is chock full of all of the nutrients you need. It is a well-rounded program that ensures you are getting all of your essentials from proteins to carbohydrates in a balanced fashion.

Eating the right kinds of foods that love your body also means that your body is better able to process them and turn them into the feel-good fuel that your body needs to stay healthy, happy and energized.

Welcome Pegans, to a whole new world.

Pegan Foods

All Pegan

Organic Fruits

Organic Vegetables

Nuts

Seeds

Healthy Oils and Butters

Nut Butters

Nut Milks

Coconut products

Limited per day

2 free-run eggs

½ cup low-glycemic whole grains

Up to ½ cup legumes

Grass-fed meats, in moderation

Free-run poultry, used as condiments

Wild fish, used as condiments

To Avoid

Dairy, processed foods and gluten-rich foods

BREAKFAST RECIPES

Coconut Pancakes with Peaches and Walnuts

Serves: 4

Preparation Time: 10 mins.

Cooking Time: 10 mins.

Ingredients

2 peaches, pitted

¼ cup organic honey, divided

¼ cup walnuts, chopped

2 eggs

¼ cup coconut flour

1 teaspoon baking powder

1 cup almond milk

½ teaspoon vanilla extract

¼ teaspoon salt

Coconut oil

Directions

1. For topping, slice peaches, mix with 2 tablespoons of honey and the walnuts, and set aside.

2. For pancakes, whisk eggs, combine with almond milk, 2 tablespoons honey, salt, vanilla extract, and 1 tablespoon of coconut oil in a bowl.
3. In a second bowl, sift coconut flour and baking powder.
4. Slowly add the wet mixture into the dry mixture while mixing.
5. Lightly coat a skillet with coconut oil and place over medium heat.
6. Pour approximately ¼ cup of batter into skillet and cook approximately 2 minutes per side. You will flip the pancakes over when little bubbles form.
7. Top with fruit and enjoy!

Nutrition (g)

Calories 366

Fat 28

Sodium 173 (mg)

Carbs 31

Sugar 24

Protein 7

Berry Coconut Shake

Serves: 2

Preparation Time: 5 mins.

Ingredients

1 cup blueberries, fresh or frozen

1 cup coconut milk

2 teaspoons flaxseed

1 teaspoon stevia

¼ cup ice

Directions

1. Combine ingredients in blender and mix until smooth.

Nutrition (g)

Calories 330

Fat 30

Sodium 20 (mg)

Carbs 19

Sugar 11

Protein 4

Eggs with Carrot and Ginger Sausage

Serves: 4

Preparation Time: 10 mins.

Cooking Time: 25 mins.

Ingredients

8 eggs, hard boiled

5 medium carrots, shredded

½ cup cauliflower florets

1 teaspoon ginger, grated

2 tablespoons coconut flour

¼ cup coconut milk

½ teaspoon vinegar

1 teaspoon salt

1 teaspoon black pepper

Coconut oil

Directions

1. Preheat oven to 400°F and lightly coat a baking pan with a little coconut oil.

2. Combine coconut milk and vinegar, let it rest for 2 minutes.

3. Combine remaining ingredients with 2 tablespoons of coconut oil in a bowl, add milk mixture.

4. Shape into small 2" sausages, place on baking pan and bake in oven for 25 minutes.
5. Serve with hard-boiled eggs.

Nutrition (g)

Calories 282

Fat 18

Sodium 198 (mg)

Carbs 14

Sugar 5

Protein 13

Pink Grapefruit with Coconut Lime Dressing

Serves: 4

Preparation Time: 5 mins.

Ingredients

2 grapefruits, segmented

¾ cup coconut milk

1 lime, juiced

½ teaspoon salt

2 tablespoons organic honey

Directions

1. Combine coconut milk, lime, salt, and honey in a bowl, mix well.
2. Divide grapefruit amongst plates, drizzle with dressing, and serve.

Nutrition (g)

Calories 156

Fat 11

Sodium 298 (mg)

Carbs 16

Sugar 15

Protein 2

Carrot Cake Smoothie

Serves: 2

Preparation Time: 5 mins.

Ingredients

2 carrots, steamed, cooled

1 tablespoon fresh ginger, grated

½ cup coconut milk

3 tablespoons honey

½ teaspoon cinnamon

½ teaspoon nutmeg

½ cup ice

Directions

1. Place ingredients in blender and mix until smooth.

Nutrition (g)

Calories 136

Fat 7

Sodium 28 (mg)

Carbs 19

Sugar 16

Protein 1

Banana Chocolate Pancakes

Serves: 4

Preparation Time: 10 mins.

Cooking Time: 10 mins.

Ingredients

2 eggs

¼ cup cocoa

2 bananas

¼ cup coconut flour

1 teaspoon baking powder

1 cup almond milk

¼ teaspoon salt

Organic honey

Coconut oil

Directions

1. For pancakes, whisk eggs in bowl and combine almond milk, 2 tablespoons honey, salt, vanilla extract and 1 tablespoon coconut oil in a bowl.

2. In a second bowl, sift coconut flour and baking powder.

3. Slowly add wet mixture into dry mixture while mixing.

4. Lightly coat a skillet with coconut oil and place over medium heat.

5. Pour approximately ¼ cup of batter into skillet and cook approximately 2 minutes per side. Flip the pancakes over when little bubbles form.
6. Slice bananas and serve on top of pancakes with a drizzle of honey.

Nutrition (g)

Calories 313

Fat 18

Sodium 58 (mg)

Carbs 38

Sugar 23

Protein 7

Spinach on Tomato Plates

Serves: 4

Preparation Time: 5 mins.

Cooking Time: 10 mins.

Ingredients

20 cups mature spinach, chopped

1 medium onion, chopped

4 tomatoes

½ teaspoon salt

½ teaspoon black pepper

Olive oil

Directions

1. Heat 3 tablespoons of olive oil in a skillet, add onion, and sauté for one minute.
2. Add spinach, salt, and black pepper, sauté until wilted.
3. Slice tomatoes, top each tomato with spinach, and serve.

Nutrition (g)

Calories 128

Fat 8

Sodium 416 (mg)

Carbs 13

Sugar 5

Protein 6

Mushroomlet

Serves: 4

Preparation Time: 10 mins.

Cooking Time: 5 mins.

Ingredients

8 eggs

3 cups button mushrooms

1 small onion, chopped

¼ cup coconut milk

½ teaspoon salt

½ teaspoon black pepper

Rapeseed oil

Directions

1. Whisk eggs in a bowl, set aside.
2. Slice mushrooms finely, combine with onion, salt, black pepper, and coconut.
3. Heat 2 teaspoons rapeseed oil in a skillet over medium-high heat, add mushrooms and onion, and sauté for 2-3 minutes until the onions are tender.
4. Add whisked eggs, cook on each side for 3 minutes.
5. Serve warm.

Nutrition (g)

Calories 239

Fat 20

Sodium 128 (mg)

Carbs 3

Sugar 2

Protein 13

Super Green Smoothie

Serves: 2

Preparation Time: 5 mins.

Ingredients

4 cups spinach

1 cup kale

1 teaspoon wheatgrass

½ cup organic orange juice

½ cup ice

Directions

1. Steam spinach and kale, cool.
2. Place ingredients in blender and mix until smooth.

Nutrition (g)

Calories 71

Fat 0

Sodium 64 (mg)

Carbs 14

Sugar 6

Protein 4

LUNCH RECIPES

Dill Zucchini Fritters

Serves: 4

Preparation Time: 15 mins.

Cooking Time: 10 mins.

Ingredients

8 small zucchinis

8 eggs

1 tablespoon coconut flour

2 tablespoons fresh dill

1 teaspoon salt

1 teaspoon black pepper

Olive oil

Directions

1. Peel and grate zucchini.
2. Whisk eggs in a large bowl, add zucchini, together with coconut flour, dill, salt, black pepper, and 2 tablespoons olive oil.
3. Heat 4 tablespoons olive oil in skillet over medium heat.
4. Drop 1 ½ tablespoons of zucchini mixture per fritter into skillet.

5. Cook each side for approximately 5 minutes.

6. Enjoy fritters alongside a green salad.

Nutrition (g)

Calories 257

Fat 17

Sodium 748 (mg)

Carbs 15

Sugar 8

Protein 16

Zucchini Quinoa Casserole

Serves: 4:

Preparation Time: 10 mins.

Cooking Time: 10 mins.

Ingredients:

8 zucchinis

1 cup quinoa

½ cup cashews

1 medium onion, diced

3 cloves garlic, minced

2 teaspoons coconut flour

1 cup coconut milk

1 teaspoon salt

1 teaspoon black pepper

Olive oil

Directions

1. Preheat oven to 400°F and lightly coat a casserole dish with a little olive oil.
2. Wash quinoa and soak in warm water for 10 minutes.
3. Cook quinoa according to package directions, but cut cooking time in half.
4. Slice 4 zucchinis into ½" thick rounds and grate the remaining zucchini (leave the skin on).

5. Heat 2 tablespoons olive oil in skillet over medium, sauté onion and garlic for one minute.
6. Combine onion mixture with quinoa, grated zucchini, coconut flour, coconut milk, salt, black pepper and spread on bottom of casserole dish.
7. Spread zucchini discs on top of grated zucchini and sprinkle cashews on top.
8. Bake for 40 minutes.

Nutrition (g)

Calories 536

Fat 33

Sodium 639 (mg)

Carbs 54

Sugar 11

Protein 15

Pistachio Jewel Salad

Serves: 4

Preparation Time: 10 mins.

Ingredients

8 ounces cooked chicken breast

4 cups green lettuce, chopped

½ cup fresh mint

1 medium pomegranate

½ cup pistachio nuts

Organic balsamic dressing

Salt

Black pepper

Directions

1. Combine salad ingredients in a bowl. Add balsamic dressing when ready to serve.

Nutrition* (g)

Calories 220

Fat 9

Sodium 72 (mg)

Carbs 14

Sugar 7

Protein 22

Analysis does not include Organic Balsamic Dressing.

Watermelon Mint Salad

Serves: 4

Preparation Time: 5 mins.

Ingredients

4 cups watermelon, cubed

¾ cup walnuts, chopped

Handful fresh mint leaves

1/2 teaspoon salt

Directions

1. Combine ingredients, refrigerate for one hour before serving.

Nutrition (g)

Calories 196

Fat 14

Sodium 297 (mg)

Carbs 15

Sugar 10

Protein 7

Hearty Cabbage and Fennel Soup

Serves: 4-6

Preparation Time: 10 mins.

Cooking Time: 7 hrs.

Ingredients

4 cups cabbage, chopped

2 fennel bulbs, stalks removed

¾ cup barley, uncooked

1 carrot, chopped

1 stalk celery, chopped

1 medium onion, chopped

4 cloves garlic, minced

6 cups filtered water

1 bay leaf½ teaspoon oregano

1 teaspoon salt

1 teaspoon black pepper

Olive oil

Directions

1. Heat 4 tablespoons olive oil in skillet over medium heat, add onion and garlic, and sauté for 1 minute. Add fennel and sauté for 3 more minutes.

2. Place onion mixture, along with remaining ingredients, in a slow cooker and cook on low for 7 hours.

Nutrition (g)

Calories 244

Fat 8

Sodium 1259 (mg)

Carbs 40

Sugar 3

Protein 7

Creamy Zucchini Soup

Serves: 4-6

Preparation Time: 10 mins.

Cooking Time: 3 hrs.

Ingredients

¾ cup red lentils

6 zucchinis, peeled and chopped

1 medium onion, chopped

4 cloves garlic, minced

1 cup coconut milk

3 cups water

1 teaspoon salt

1 teaspoon black pepper

Olive oil

Directions

1. Soak red lentils in warm water for 20 minutes.
2. Heat 4 tablespoons olive oil in skillet over medium.
3. Add garlic and onion, sauté for one minute.
4. Rinse lentils and place in slow cooker, along with onion, garlic, zucchini, water, and salt. Cook on high for 3 hours.

5. Stir in coconut milk and cook for another 20 minutes.

6. Using an immersion blender, mix until smooth.

Nutrition (g)

Calories 258

Fat 15

Sodium 803 (mg)

Carbs 26

Sugar 6

Protein 10

Citrus Avocado Salad

Serves: 4

Preparation Time: 10 mins.

Ingredients

8 ounces pasture-raised chicken breast

2 oranges

1 avocado, pitted and sliced

½ cup almonds, chopped

4 cups lettuce, chopped

½ teaspoon salt

½ teaspoon black pepper

Directions

1. Peel and segment oranges, combine with avocado, walnut, salt, and black pepper.
2. Plate lettuce, top with the orange-avocado mixture.
3. Shred chicken breast with fork and divide evenly among salad plates.

Nutrition (g)

Calories 315

Fat 18

Sodium 72 (mg)

Carbs 19

Sugar 10

Protein 23

The Pegan Wrap

Serves: 6

Preparation Time: 10 mins.

Cooking Time: 10 mins.

Ingredients

1 ½ cups almond flour

½ teaspoon salt

½ teaspoon baking powder

¾ cup water

Rapeseed oil

Filling

2 cups white kidney beans

4 red, yellow, and green bell peppers, seeded and sliced

1 red onion, sliced

½ cup walnuts, chopped

1 teaspoon oregano

1 teaspoon salt

1 teaspoon black pepper

Olive oil

Directions

1. Combine flour, salt, and baking powder in a bowl, slowly add water, mixing to form a ball.

2. Knead dough on flat surface, and divide into 6 balls.
3. Use a rolling pin to roll out the tortillas.
4. Heat non-stick pan on medium, and cook tortillas for 2 minutes per side.
5. For the filling heat 4 tablespoons olive oil in skillet, add onions, sauté for a minute, add bell peppers and sauté for 5 minutes.
6. Sprinkle with salt, black pepper, and oregano. Fill wraps and serve.

Nutrition (g)

Calories 441

Fat 19

Sodium 213 (mg)

Carbs 50

Sugar 7

Protein 21

Creamy Cauliflower and Chicken Breast

Serves: 4

Preparation Time: 5 mins.

Cooking Time: 35 mins.

Ingredients

8 ounces pasture-raised chicken breast, cubed

1 large head cauliflower

2 large carrots, sliced into discs

1 cup coconut milk

1 teaspoon paprika

1 teaspoon salt

Coconut oil

Directions

1. Preheat oven to 400°F and lightly coat a casserole dish with a little coconut oil.
2. Slice cauliflower into florets and mix with carrot discs, salt, and paprika.
3. Place cauliflower in casserole dish and pour coconut milk on top.
4. Cover with aluminum foil, and bake for 35 minutes.

5. For the chicken, heat 3 tablespoons coconut oil in skillet, add chicken breast cubes and sauté for 7 minutes, or until no longer pink inside.
6. Enjoy chicken breast pieces along with creamy cauliflower.

Nutrition (g)

Calories 319

Fat 23

Sodium 115 (mg)

Carbs 10

Sugar 5

Protein 21

Watermelon Mint Salad

Serves: 4

Preparation Time: 5 mins.

Ingredients

4 cups watermelon, cubed

¾ cup walnuts, choppedHandful fresh mint leaves1/2 teaspoon salt

Directions

1. Combine ingredients, refrigerate for one hour before serving.

Nutrition (g)

Calories 196

Fat 14

Sodium 297 (mg)

Carbs 15

Sugar 10

Protein 7

DINNER RECIPES

Stuffed Peppers

Serves: 4

Preparation Time: 10 mins.

Cooking Time: 25 mins.

Ingredients

12 ounces grass-fed lean ground beef

4 green bell peppers

1 cup cauliflower, grated

¼ cup sundried tomato

1 medium onion, minced

4 cloves garlic, minced

2 cups tomato puree

1 teaspoon oregano

½ teaspoon cinnamon

1 teaspoon salt

1 teaspoon black pepper

Olive oil

Directions

1. Heat 2 tablespoons olive oil in skillet, add onion and garlic and sauté for one minute.
2. Place half of the mixture into a slow cooker, along with tomato puree, and mix.

3. Add beef to skillet, brown, and drain.

4. Mix beef and onion with grated cauliflower and sundried tomatoes, salt, black pepper, cinnamon, and oregano.

5. Slice the tops off the peppers, remove seeds, and stuff peppers with cauliflower mixture.

6. Place peppers in the slow cooker and cook on low for 7 hours.

Nutrition (g)

Calories 334

Fat 15

Sodium 692 (mg)

Carbs 27

Sugar 14

Protein 23

Pesto Noodles

Serves: 4

Preparation Time: 10 mins.

Ingredients

2 cups basil, fresh

3 tablespoon pine nuts

2 cloves garlic

6 zucchinis

Salt

Black pepper

Extra virgin olive oil

Directions

1. Using a mandolin slicer, make long noodles of zucchini.
2. Place in a mixing bowl, and stir in 4 tablespoons extra virgin olive oil and ½ teaspoon salt, set aside.
3. Combine basil, pine nuts, ½ teaspoon salt, ½ teaspoon black pepper, and 1/3 cup extra virgin olive oil in a blender, and mix until smooth.
4. Serve pesto over zucchini noodles.

Nutrition (g)

Calories 156

Fat 12

Sodium 69 (mg)

Carbs 12

Sugar 5

Protein 5

Chick Peas with Veggie and Bean Sprout Sauté

Serves: 4

Preparation Time: 10 mins.

Cooking Time: 10 mins.

Ingredients

2 cups chick peas, cooked

1 cup broccoli florets

1 cup cauliflower florets

1 carrot, sliced

1 stalk celery, diced

1 medium onion, sliced

4 cloves garlic, minced

3 cups bean sprouts

1 teaspoon black pepper

½ cup coconut aminos

Olive oil

Directions

1. Heat 4 tablespoons olive oil in skillet, add onion, garlic, and sauté for one minute.
2. Add veggies, except bean sprouts, and sauté for 5 minutes or until tender.
3. Add bean sprouts and sauté for another 3 minutes. Mix in coconut aminos.

4. Divide sprout mixture among plates, top with chick peas, and serve.

Nutrition (g)

Calories 293

Fat 9

Sodium 426 (mg)

Carbs 43

Sugar 2

Protein 13

Lavender Zucchini Wrap

Serves: 4

Preparation Time: 10 mins.

Cooking Time: 20 mins.

Ingredients

4 zucchinis

¼ cup lavender flowers

½ teaspoon salt

½ teaspoon black pepper

Coconut oil, melted

4 Pegan Wraps (recipe in breakfasts)

Directions:

1. Slice zucchinis in half.
2. Combine lavender flowers, salt, black pepper, and 4 tablespoon coconut oil.
3. Place zucchini in marinade and let sit for one hour.
4. Heat grill to medium-high, and cook zucchinis for 3 minutes per side.

Nutrition (g)

Calories 211

Fat 18

Sodium 605 (mg)

Carbs 11

Sugar 4

Protein 4

Grilled Portabella Mushrooms Salad

Serves: 4

Preparation Time: 10 mins.

Cooking Time: 10 mins.

Ingredients

4 portabella mushrooms

2 cups quinoa, cooked and cooled

4 garlic cloves, minced

3 cups arugula

2 cups green lettuce

2 red bell peppers, julienned

Balsamic dressing

Salt

Black pepper

Extra virgin olive oil

Directions

1. Combine 4 tablespoons extra virgin olive oil with garlic and ½ teaspoon salt, brush portabella mushroom, refrigerate for one hour.

2. Combine quinoa, arugula, green lettuce, and bell peppers, set aside.

3. Heat grill to medium-high, grill portabella mushrooms.

4. Drizzle salad with balsamic dressing and serve with garlicky mushrooms

Nutrition (g)

Calories 154

Fat 12

Sodium 47 (mg)

Carbs 10

Sugar 6

Protein 2

Asparagus Sauté

Serves: 4

Preparation Time: 10 mins.

Cooking Time: 15 mins.

Ingredients

12 ounces grass-fed beef steak

16 asparagus spears

2 cups cherry tomatoes

½ cup almonds

6 cloves garlic

¼ cup coconut aminos

½ teaspoon cayenne pepper

Salt

Olive oil

Directions

1. Slice each asparagus spear into thirds.
2. Heat 4 tablespoons olive oil in skillet over medium, add garlic, and sauté for one minute.
3. Add asparagus and sauté for 4 minutes.
4. Add tomato, cayenne pepper, and almonds, sauté everything for 5 minutes.
5. Mix in coconut aminos, turn heat to low, cover for 5 minutes.

6. For beef, heat grill to high, salt steak and cook each side for 4 minutes for medium rare, serve with asparagus.

Nutrition (g)

Calories 254

Fat 16

Sodium 106 (mg)

Carbs 322

Sugar 3

Protein 23

Wild Salmon and Cashewed Plums

Serves: 4

Preparation Time: 5 mins.

Cooking Time: 25 mins.

Ingredients

4 4 ounce wild caught salmon fillets

8 plums, halved and seeded

¾ cup cashews, chopped

1 teaspoon salt

1 teaspoon black pepper

4 cups Romaine lettuce

1 red onion, sliced

Balsamic vinaigrette

Olive oil

Directions

1. Preheat oven to 400°F and lightly coat 2 oven-safe glass baking dishes with olive oil.

2. Sprinkle salmon with salt, and place in one casserole dish.

3. Place plums in second casserole dish and sprinkle with salt, black pepper, and cashews, drizzle with a little olive oil.

4. Slide both dishes into the oven, bake plums for 25 minutes and salmon for 12 minutes. Turn salmon halfway through.

5. Combine lettuce, red onion, and 4 tablespoon balsamic vinaigrette in a bowl, divide amongst 4 plates.

6. Place a salmon fillet and 2 plums on each plate and serve.

Nutrition (g)

Calories 402

Fat 23

Sodium 790 (mg)

Carbs 24

Sugar 18

Protein 27

Baked Eggplants in Tomato Sauce

Serves: 4

Preparation Time: 10 mins.

Cooking Time: 40 mins.

Ingredients:

4 eggplants

4 tomatoes, quartered

3 cups tomato puree

1 onion, finely chopped

4 cloves garlic, minced

1 teaspoon oregano

Salt

Black pepper

Olive oil

Directions

1. Slice eggplants in half and sprinkle with salt. Let the eggplants rest at room temperature for 20-30 minutes, until they have sweat some water out. Pat dry with paper towel, removing all excess water and salt.

2. Preheat oven to 400°F, brush a casserole dish with olive oil.

3. Mix tomato with salt, and black pepper to taste. Add oregano, garlic, and onion, and pour into casserole dish.
4. Place eggplants in casserole dish, face down, and bake in oven for 20 minutes.
5. Remove from oven, turn eggplant over, cover with aluminum foil, and bake for another 20 minutes or until the eggplants are fork tender.

Nutrition (g)

Calories 308

Fat 9

Sodium 362 (mg)

Carbs 58

Sugar 30

Protein 10

APPETIZER RECIPES

Almond Honey Cauliflower Skewers

Serves: 4

Preparation Time: 10 mins.

Cooking Time: 12 mins.

Ingredients

½ cup organic almond butter

1 medium head cauliflower

2 tablespoons honey

½ teaspoon salt

Directions

1. Separate cauliflower into florets, trim stems.
2. Combine almond butter, honey, and salt in a bowl.
3. Add cauliflower, and coat with dressing.
4. Place 4 cauliflower florets per skewer.
5. Heat grill to medium-high.
6. Place skewers on grill and cook for 12 minutes over indirect heat, be sure to turn as required.

Nutrition (g)

Calories 266

Fat 18

Sodium 334 (mg)

Carbs 22

Sugar 12

Protein 10

Garlicky Red Bell Pepper Hummus

Serves: 4

Preparation Time: 10 mins.

Ingredients

4 red bell peppers, seeded

2 cups cauliflower florets

6 cloves garlic

½ teaspoon salt

½ teaspoon black pepper

Extra virgin olive oil

Directions

1. Place ingredients in a blender and mix until fairly smooth but with some texture.
2. Serve with fresh veggies.

Nutrition (g)

Calories 117

Fat 7

Sodium 311 (mg)

Carbs 12

Sugar 6

Protein 3

Cashew Raisin Nut Dip

Serves: 6

Preparation Time: 5 mins.

Ingredients

1 cup cashews, divided

¼ cup raisins

¼ cup coconut milk

¼ cup filtered water

Directions

1. Place ¾ cup cashews, coconut milk, and filtered water in blender, mix until smooth.
2. Chop remaining cashews, combine with raisins and fold into cashew coconut mixture.
3. Serve with fruit.

Nutrition (g)

Calories 172

Fat 13

Sodium 6 (mg)

Carbs 13

Sugar 5

Protein 4

Grapefruit Sorbet

Serves: 4

Preparation Time: 10 mins.

Cooking Time: 25 mins.

Ingredients

2 grapefruits, peeled and segmented

4 mint leaves.

3 tablespoon clover honey

Directions

1. Place ingredients in a blender and mix until smooth.
2. Pour mixture into a metal container, cover and place in freezer for 2 hours.
3. Remove from freezer and beat for 2 minutes. Return to freezer for 5 more hours.

Nutrition (g)

Calories 17

Fat 0

Sodium 0 (mg)

Carbs 4

Sugar 3

Protein 1

Pecan and Grape Bites

Serves: 6

Preparation Time: 5 mins.

Cooking Time: 0 mins.

Ingredients

½ cup pecans

4 cups green grapes

½ teaspoon salt

Directions

1. Place pecans and salt in blender, mix until smooth.
2. Slice grapes in half lengthwise, spread a little pecan on one half and place other half on top.

Nutrition (g)

Calories 173

Fat 14

Sodium 195 (mg)

Carbs 13

Sugar 11

Protein 2

DESSERT RECIPES

Chocolate Coffee Cake

Serves: 8

Preparation Time: 10 mins.

Cooking Time: 30 mins.

Ingredients

1 cup cocoa powder

1 cup tapioca flour

¼ cup coconut flour

½ cup walnuts, chopped

6 Medjool dates, pitted

1 cup almond milk

½ cup brewed coffee

1 teaspoon vanilla extract

1 teaspoon baking powder

1 teaspoon vinegar

¼ teaspoon salt

½ cup coconut oil

Directions

1. Preheat oven to 400°F and coat a 9x13-inch baking pan with a little coconut oil.
2. Place dates in food processor and mix into paste.

3. Combine dates with wet ingredients in one bowl and beat.

4. Mix dry ingredients together in a separate bowl, slowly add to wet mixture while beating.

5. Pour batter into prepared cake tray and bake in oven for 30 minutes.

Nutrition (g)

Calories 446

Fat 27

Sodium 92 (mg)

Carbs 53

Sugar 15

Protein 6

Strawberry Cashew Surprise

Serves: 8

Preparation Time: 15 mins.

Ingredients

4 cups strawberries, hulled

1 cup coconut cream (from can)

1 ½ cups cashews, divided

6 Medjool Dates

1/2 teaspoon vanilla

Directions

1. Place half the cashews in a food processor and crush into butter, add coconut cream and vanilla, and mix. Remove from blender, refrigerate.
2. Clean blender, add remaining cashews and dates, mix until crumbly.
3. Pat cashew-date mixture into bottom of 8" pie plate and place in the freezer for one hour.
4. Slice strawberries.
5. Scoop cashew coconut cream into 8" pie plate, top with strawberries and refrigerate for 2 hours before serving.

Nutrition (g)

Calories 191

Fat 15

Sodium 8 (mg)

Carbs 13

Sugar 5

Protein 4

Pistachio Cookies

Serves: 16

Preparation Time: 10 mins.

Cooking Time: 15 mins.

Ingredients

½ cup pistachios, chopped

1 cup almond meal

8 Medjool Dates, pitted

½ teaspoon baking soda

½ teaspoon salt

2 tablespoons coconut oil, melted

¼ cup filtered water

Directions

1. Place Medjool dates and water in blender, and mix until paste forms.
2. Preheat oven to 375°F and line a baking sheet with parchment paper.
3. Combine ingredients in bowl.
4. Drop a spoonful of mixture at a time on baking sheet and bake for 15 minutes.

Nutrition (g)

Calories 94

Fat 5

Sodium 112 (mg)

Carbs 12

Sugar 9

Protein 2

Carrot Nut Mini-Muffins

Serves: 24

Preparation Time: 10 mins.

Cooking Time: 20 mins.

Ingredients

¼ cup coconut flour

½ cup walnuts, chopped

2 carrots, grated

½ teaspoon cinnamon

1 cup almond milk

1 teaspoon vinegar

3 teaspoons Stevia

¼ teaspoon salt

2 tablespoons coconut oil

Directions

1. Preheat oven to 375°F and line a mini muffin tray with muffin liners.
2. Combine almond milk and vinegar, allow to sit for a few minutes.
3. Combine dry ingredients in one bowl.
4. Add vanilla and carrots to almond mixture.
5. Slowly add dry ingredients to the bowl while continuously mixing.
6. Fill muffin cups and bake for 20 minutes.

Nutrition (g)

Calories 59

Fat 5

Sodium 32 (mg)

Carbs 2

Sugar 1

Protein 1

CONCLUSION

If you're looking for an ethical, holistic way of eating then you've found it with the Pegan diet. The principles of the Paleo diet mean you are eating fresh food from the land while Veganism encourages the same thing minus the animal protein.

Peganism allows you to enjoy delicious, satisfying whole foods while still allowing for a little ethically-raised meat protein, low-glycemic grains and legumes on the side. The wide range of foods allowed on the Pegan diet make it a functional lifestyle choice that you can stick to without ever feeling deprived.

Eating the Pegan way means you'll be feeling happy, energetic, and most importantly, you'll feel really great about the fantastic choices you are making.

OTHER BOOKS FROM MADISON MILLER

To check a book, just click on the cover.

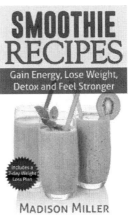

APPENDIX

Cooking Conversion Charts

1. Volumes

US Fluid Oz.	US	US Dry Oz.	Metric Liquid ml
¼ oz.	2 tsp.	1 oz.	10 ml.
½ oz.	1 Tbsp.	2 oz.	15 ml.
1 oz.	2 Tbsp.	3 oz.	30 ml.
2 oz.	¼ cup	3½ oz.	60 ml.
4 oz.	½ cup	4 oz.	125 ml.
6 oz.	¾ cup	6 oz.	175 ml.
8 oz.	1 cup	8 oz.	250 ml.

Tsp.= teaspoon - Tbsp.= tablespoon – oz.= ounce – ml.= millimeter

2. Oven Temperatures

Celsius (°C)*	Fahrenheit (°F)
90	220
110	225
120	250
140	275
150	300
160	325
180	350
190	375
200	400
215	425
230	450
250	475
260	500

*Rounded figures

Made in the USA
Middletown, DE
06 July 2018